Poleroid Theatre in association with Mercury Theatre
presents

PLASTIC

by Kenneth Emson

Plastic was first performed at the Old Red Lion Theatre,
Islington, on 3 April 2018 before transferring to the
Mercury Theatre, Colchester, on 26 April 2018.

PLASTIC

by Kenneth Emson

CAST

KEV	Mark Weinman
BEN	Thomas Coombes
JACK	Louis Greatorex
LISA	Madison Clare

CREATIVE TEAM

Director	Josh Roche
Designer	Sophie Thomas
Lighting Designer	Peter Small
Sound Designer	Kieran Lucas
Stage Manager	Kieran Lucas
PR	Chloé Nelkin Consulting
Poster Image	Helen Murray
Producer	Molly Roberts, Poleroid Theatre
Associate Producer	Corinne Salisbury
Assistant Producer	Holly White

ACKNOWLEDGEMENTS

A work-in-progress version of the play was performed at Latitude Festival, Suffolk, on 14 July 2015, with thanks to actors Scott Hazell, Adam Gillen, James Cooney and Katie Bonna.

Poleroid would also like to thank The Mercury Theatre team, Split Infinitive Trust, The Old Vic Workrooms, Tom Wright and The Old Vic team, Vicky Graham, Nick Rampley and Morley College, Creative Prospects and students of Big Creative Education, James Grieve, Joe Price, Jon McLeod, Sarah Jane Leigh, Will Howard, Kate Lamb, Rikki Lawton, Mark Allinson, Andrea Stark, Pauline Tambling, Collective, Julie Roberts, Bransby Roberts, Mick Fox and Mathew Foster.

Alongside the original production of *Plastic*, Poleroid are proud to have offered a number of outreach opportunities for young people and emerging artists. Thanks to all the drama schools, colleges and universities who have engaged with these activities. *Plastic* can be found as a set text on the BA Contemporary Plays & Playwrights course 2018 at St Mary's University.

Plastic is generously supported by Arts Council England, Royal Victoria Hall Foundation, Blyth Watson Charitable Trust, The Old Vic, Jocelyn Abbey and Triple E Ltd.

Triple E Ltd, the industry leading designer and manufacturer of stage tracking and engineering products is delighted to support Poleroid Theatre's innovative staging of *Plastic*.

Triple E Ltd

POLEROID THEATRE

Run by actor and Artistic Director Molly Roberts, who was one of The Old Vic 12 for 2016-2017 and a Stage One New Producer, Poleroid Theatre are a new-writing theatre company and pioneers of Artist Development.

Poleroid discover, curate and give a platform to fast-rising emerging writers, actors and directors from across the UK. Their collaborative method gives writers the vital time and space to work practically alongside a director and professional actors to create bold, current, high-quality new theatre work which pushes the boundaries of form and style. They then bring this work to areas of low cultural engagement across the nation with a range of outreach opportunities specifically designed for young people.

In 2014 they were nominated for three Off-West End Theatre Awards for their production of *Free Fall* by Vinay Patel, published by Methuen Drama. Their production of *This Must Be The Place* by Brad Birch and Kenneth Emson (Latitude 2016 and Vault Festival 2017) received 4* and 5* reviews and won Vault's Show of the Year Award; the script is published by Nick Hern Books. Other work includes *The Locker Outings* (five new plays by Vinay Patel, Sarah Kosar, Jonathan Schey, Helen Russell-Clark & Andrew Thompson for Vault Festival); *The Allotment* by Andrew Thompson (Live Theatre, supported by Arts Council England); *Bangin' Wolves* by Phoebe Éclair-Powell and *Life On A Plum* by Luke Barnes (Wilderness Festival). Poleroid also produce Write It : Mic It, an acclaimed eclectic performance platform which has given opportunities to over 200 established and emerging artists from across the UK since 2012 and has been hosted at the Paines Plough Roundabout, Live Theatre, Vault Festival, Hackney Attic, Ritzy Brixton, Castle Hotel Manchester, Wilderness Festival and Standon Calling Festival.

www.poleroidtheatre.co.uk
@PoleroidTheatre

THE MERCURY THEATRE

The Mercury Theatre Colchester is the most active producing theatre in East Anglia, and it is a vital centre of excellence in the East's growing creative economy.

Rooted in its local community, the theatre touches over 130,000 people in Colchester and the surrounding area each year through the vibrant and broad programme we stage across two auditoria, and through community education partnerships.

Under the Made in Colchester brand, the Mercury creates theatre which reaches audiences and generates critical attention regionally and nationally. The Mercury is a champion of regional arts, both as an active co-producer with other venues and companies and also touring our own productions to audiences across the UK.

Our Main Theatre seats just under 500, while our newly refurbished Studio Theatre seats 98. On-site production and workshop facilities create sets, props and costumes for both in-house productions and touring companies, including Talawa and the National Theatre.

In 2016, the Mercury was starting house for Paul Taylor-Mills' tour of *End of the Rainbow*, produced a UK tour of *Clybourne Park*, and co-produced *Sweeney Todd* with Derby Theatre. Last year, we co-produced John Cleese's adaptation of a farce by Georges Feydeau, *Bang Bang*, while the Made in Colchester and English Touring Theatre production of *The Weir* toured nationally throughout autumn and winter 2017. This spring we co-produce new British musical *Pieces of String* with TBO Productions.

www.mercurytheatre.co.uk
@mercurytheatre

CAST

MADISON CLARE | LISA
Madison is a recent LAMDA Acting graduate. *Plastic* marks Madison's professional stage debut. Theatre credits whilst training include: *A Midsummer Night's Dream, A Comedy of Errors, Women on the Verge of a Nervous Breakdown, No Quarter, Blood Wedding* and *The Dark Things*. Other theatre credits include: *War Whores* (Courtyard Theatre); *Close* (Landor Space).

THOMAS COOMBES | BEN
Thomas trained at Guildford School of Acting. Theatre credits include: *King Lear* (Royal Exchange Theatre, Manchester); *Barbarians* (Tooting Art's Club/West End); *Single Spies* (Rose, Kingston); *The Merchant of Venice* (Shakespeare's Globe); *Finding Alice* (Lyric Hammersmith/ Tricycle). Television credits include: *Save Me* (Sky Atlantic); *Hatton Garden, Endeavour, Prime Suspect: 1973, Jekyll and Hyde, Life of Crime* (ITV); *Lucky Man* (Sky One); *Knightfall* (History); *Silent Witness, Cuffs, The Scandalous Lady W, Wallander, Count Arthur Strong, Atlantis, The Honourable Woman, Him & Her: The Wedding, Doctors, The Genius of Turner, EastEnders* (BBC); *Man Down* (CH4); *Suspects* (CH5).

LOUIS GREATOREX | JACK
Louis trained at Nottingham Television Workshop. Credits include: *Safe* (Netflix); *The Last Post, Last Tango In Halifax Series 1-4* (BBC). *Plastic* marks Louis's professional stage debut.

MARK WEINMAN | KEV
Mark studied Drama at the University of Manchester. As an actor his theatre credits include: *So Here We Are, Mr Noodles* (Royal Exchange Theatre, Manchester); *Captain Amazing* (Soho/Live/UK tour); *Prime Time, The Bash, Serjeant Musgrave's Dance* (Royal Court); *Still Killing Time, Eating Ice Cream on Gaza Beach* (Soho); *Herons* (Stephen Joseph/Manchester Library Theatre); *Fastburn* (KneeHigh); *The Hairy Ape* (Southwark Playhouse); *The Emperor Jones* (National Theatre); *Barrow Hill* (Finborough); *Edmond* (Theatre Royal Haymarket), *Step 9 (of 12)* (New Britannia), *Sandy 123* (The Roundhouse); *Amphibians* (Offstage Theatre) and *Sherlock Holmes* (Italy national tour). Television and film credits include: *Press, The Gamechangers, Episodes* (BBC), *Back, Humans, The People Next Door, The Guilt Trip* (CH4); *Sex Ed* (Stan & Lola Films); *Burning* (Tantrum Films). As a writer his credits include: *DYL* (Old Red Lion); *Sex Ed* (Stan & Lola Films).

CREATIVE TEAM

KENNETH EMSON | WRITER
Kenneth Emson is an award-winning writer for stage and screen.
His plays have been performed at venues including the Bush Theatre
(*Terrorism*), the Mercury Theatre (*Quadrophenia*), Sir John Mills
(*Parkway Dreams*) and Tristan Bates (*Whispering Happiness*), as well at
festivals in the UK, Croatia, New York and Cape Town. His recent play
for Poleroid Theatre, *This Must Be The Place*, co-written with Brad
Birch won Show of the Year Award at Vault Festival. He has written for
EastEnders, *Doctors*, BBC Radio 3 and 4. He was co-creator, co-writer
and associate producer on the BAFTA Craft, SXSW, Broadcast and
Prix Italia nominated *Last Hours of Laura K*, and adapted the Agatha
Christie short story *The Coming of Mr Quin* (BAFTA CYMRU nominated).
He has been shortlisted for the Bruntwood and Red Planet Prizes as
well as winning the Adrienne Benham, Off West End – Adopt a
Playwright and Mercury Theatre Essex Playwriting Awards.

JOSH ROCHE | DIRECTOR
Josh Roche is the winner of the JMK Award 2017, directing *My Name is
Rachel Corrie* at the Young Vic Theatre. From 2011-2016 Josh was the
Artistic Director of Fat Git Theatre and is currently Associate Director
with Poleroid Theatre. His work with Fat Git Theatre included new work
from writers such as George Saunders, Howard Brenton, Joe White and
Laura Jacqmin, produced at Soho Theatre, Theatre503, the New
Diorama, Warwick Arts Centre and across the Edinburgh Festival Fringe.
Josh is the previous Writers' Centre Associate at the Soho Theatre and an
Associate Reader for Sonia Friedman Productions. Josh has worked as an
assistant director with John Dove, Gregory Doran, Polly Findlay, Maria
Aberg, Joe Murphy and Steve Marmion. He has directed one-off events
for Shakespeare's Globe and the Royal Shakespeare Company. He was an
associate director for nabokov in the UK and Off-Broadway and is an
Educational Associate Practitioner with the RSC.

SOPHIE THOMAS | DESIGNER
Sophie Thomas is a UK-based set and costume designer working in
theatre, film and live events. She completed a residency at the Royal
Shakespeare Company as Assistant Designer 2015-16. Design credits for
theatre include: *My Name Is Rachel Corrie* (Young Vic, 2017); *Herons*,
The Imaginary Misogynist (Guildhall School of Music and Drama, 2016);
The Slave (Tristan Bates, 2016); *Henry V* (Cambridge Arts Theatre,
2015). Film credits include: *Carnage: Swallowing the Past* (BBC, 2017);
New Gods (Jack Burke Films 2016); *Never Land* (Union Pictures, 2016);
Ringo (Jack Burke Films, 2015); *The Listener* (Good Shout, 2014). Live:
Bas: *Too High To Riot* (US tour 2016); *Maribou State* (Koko, 2016); *The
Hics* (Oslo Hackney, 2014).

PETER SMALL | LIGHTING DESIGNER

Peter studied Lighting Design at RADA. So far in 2018 he has been nominated for two Off West End Best Lighting Awards for *A Girl In School Uniform (walks in to a bar)* at the New Diorama and *Black Mountain* for Paines Plough at the Orange Tree Theatre. Recent lighting designs for theatre include: *Old Fools* (Southwark Playhouse); *Out of Love*, *Black Mountain* and *How To Be A Kid* (Paines Plough Roundabout national tour/ Orange Tree), *A Girl In School Uniform (walks into a bar)* (New Diorama); *FOX* (Old Red Lion); *Memory of Leaves* (UK tour); *She Called Me Mother* (Pitch Lake Productions, UK tour); *The Venus Factor* (Bridewell/MTA Academy); *Electric*, *Politrix* (Big House Theatre); *East End Boys and West End Girls* (Arcola/UK tour); *A Midsummer Night's Dream*, *Free Association* and *Crazy Lady* (Forum Alpbach, Austria); *Never Such Innocence* (Australia House, London); *Almost Near* (Finborough); *Richard III*, *Bard on Board 2* (Royal Court, Queen Mary 2 Ocean Liner). Lighting designs for Musical Theatre include: *All Or Nothing* (West End/UK national tours/ Crescent/Vaults); *Cinderella* (Loughborough Theatre); *Tom & Jerry* (EventBox Theatre, Egypt); *The Venus Factor* (Bridewell).

KIERAN LUCAS | SOUND DESIGNER & STAGE MANAGER

Kieran Lucas is a London based sound designer and theatre-maker, founding member of Barrel Organ and associate artist with Coney. Recent credits include: *My Name is Rachel Corrie* (Young Vic); *Anyone's Guess How We Got Here* (ZOO Venues/CPT); *Hear Me Raw* (Soho/ Underbelly); *Elsa* (Soho/Assembly); *BIG GUNS* (The Yard); *I am Fortune. You Are Dark Candy* (Exeter Bike Shed/tour); *Your Connection Is Not Private* (Free Word Centre); *Blasted* (Styx); *This Must Be The Place* (Poleroid Theatre/Vaults); *Grown Up* (CPT); *REMOTE* (CPT/tour); *Under the Skin* (St Paul's Cathedral); *Spanish Tragedy* (Old Red Lion); *A Third* (Finborough); *Some People Talk About Violence* (Summerhall/tour).

MOLLY ROBERTS | PRODUCER

Molly Roberts is a professional actor and Artistic Director of Poleroid Theatre. As a producer she specialises in working collaboratively with new writing and developing emerging artists. In 2017 she was attached to The Old Vic Theatre as one of The Old Vic 12 and is a Stage One New Producer. Her Latitude Festival production of *This Must Be The Place* by Brad Birch & Kenneth Emson sold out at Vault Festival 2017 and won their Show of the Year Award; the script is published by Nick Hern Books. Her 2014 production of *Free Fall* by Vinay Patel (BBC's *Murdered By My Father*) was nominated for three Off West End Theatre Awards; the script is published by Methuen Drama. She has also produced shows with the Soho Theatre, Paines Plough Roundabout, Orange Tree Theatre, Young Vic JMK Award and her acclaimed new-writing night *Write It : Mic It* has played at Live Theatre, Paines Plough Roundabout, Vault Festival, Hackney Attic, Castle Hotel Manchester, Wilderness Festival, Standon Calling. As an actor she has been nominated for Best Female Performance at the Off West End Theatre Awards and works regularly across theatre and television. Acting credits include: Chichester/Royal Lyceum production of *Pressure* (UK tour/Park Theatre); *Jumping Puddles* (Frantic Assembly/Open Clasp); *Anna of the Five Towns* and *The Snow Queen* (New Vic Theatre), BBC & Channel 4 amongst others and she graduated from the Guildford School of Acting in 2011.

CORINNE SALISBURY | ASSOCIATE PRODUCER

Corinne Salisbury is an independent theatre producer based in Edinburgh. From 2013-2015 she worked full-time as shared General Manager (funded by the Paul Hamlyn Foundation) for a consortium of four new-writing theatre companies, all Associate Companies of Paines Plough, including nabokov, Forward Theatre Project and Theatre Uncut. Since going freelance in 2015 she has worked as a producer, consultant, tour-booker and fundraiser, predominantly for smaller theatre companies producing innovative and socially-engaged new writing. She has lead-produced studio productions in London and also on tour throughout the UK: including the world premiere of *Genesis* by Frazer Flintham, and Jane Upton's George Devine Award-winning play *All The Little Lights*. Companies she has worked with in a freelance capacity include the Finborough Theatre, the Bush Theatre, Forward Theatre Project, Fifth Word Theatre, Poleroid Theatre, Bad Physics, Theatre Uncut, Sheer Drop, Notnow Collective, Les Enfants Terribles and Tangled Feet.

HOLLY WHITE | ASSISTANT PRODUCER

Holly is a theatre producer specialising in new writing. She has recently produced shows at VAULT Festival, New Diorama Theatre and the Edinburgh Fringe and has worked with companies including Rive Productions & Talawa Theatre Company. Holly is currently Assistant Producer at HighTide.

PLASTIC

Kenneth Emson

Acknowledgements

Thanks to Jodi and Declan. Sarah Liisa and the rest of the team at Nick Hern. Emily, Georgie and Tumi at The Agency. Brad, Luke, Jon, Rachel, Anya, Dan, Nat, Darwen and Marcelo who listen to me moan and keep me sane. Sofie Mason and Disco Di for everything. And Angela, for putting up with me.

K.E.

For AK Dancer
and the girl who wanted to be a ballerina.
Nothing without you

Characters

KEV, *late thirties (nineteen)*
BEN, *mid-thirties (fifteen)*
JACK, *fifteen*
LISA, *fifteen*

The play is set in a small town along the Thames Estuary in Essex.

Author's Note

Punctuation is used to mark delivery in performance not to conform to the rules of grammar.

(/) means the next speech begins at that point.

(–) means the next line or thought interrupts what is currently being said.

(…) at the end of a speech means it trails off.

Lines enclosed in speech marks are when characters play someone else; this should be marked in delivery.

Lines in italics are spoken as active dialogue between characters.

Blank space in between lines indicates a length of time between speech.

This text went to press before the end of rehearsals and so may differ slightly from the play as performed.

KEV   So it's two-all.
Last minute of the Cup Final
The All-Essex Cup Final

BEN   Big deal

KEV   The pitch is heavy and wet
Kits are sodden with a mix of mud
Sweat
And blood.

BEN   We stand on the sideline
Like a couple of mugs
Blazers masking our shrugs

KEV   First years

BEN   Too young

KEV   Too dumb
To understand.

BEN   Just the kids from Colville Close
Where it's small
Where it's close.

KEV   Recently promoted from Primary

BEN   Where you could still be

KEV   Kids.

BEN   But not here.
Not now.

'GO ON LAD!'

Someone shouts from the touchline

KEV   As the small kid from Year 10 cuts in past their left back

BEN   Takes the ball into the penalty area

KEV   Raises his left foot

BEN   Looks at the goal

KEV   Imagines the school assembly dedicated to him

BEN   The girls in their white shirts

KEV   Moist at the mention of his name

BEN   The Year 11s that never noticed him
       Except to throw stolen pool balls at him

KEV   When he hadn't found out the importance

BEN   Of kicking a ball into an empty net

KEV   And the friends it can get –

BEN   You.

KEV   Rain
       Stops
       On
       Cue.
       And time enters
       Slow motion
       Action replay
       Sky Sports
       Andy Gray
       Time to have a little scratch around at the grey matter
       Interlude.
       As in that one moment
       When he has the ball at his feet
       The goal in his sights

       His life…
       His whole life in his sights…

BEN   Then –

KEV   BANG

BEN   Their centre back comes crashing through him not
       coming close to the ball

KEV   Alan Hansen's saying
       'Disgraceful'

BEN   The ref's whistle pierces the air

KEV   Alan Hansen's saying
        'No danger'

BEN   The ref that is in fact our PE teacher Mr Power

KEV   Alan Hansen's saying
        'Stonewall'

BEN   Who was never going to not give the penalty in
        a million years

KEV   Was he?

BEN   'What happened to the golden generation?'
        Alan Hansen's still / saying

KEV   But one lad ain't a kid

BEN   On this pitch where dreams are made.

KEV   One lad ain't shaking

BEN   Hands quaking

KEV   Nerves faking.

BEN   One lad just knows that it's his time

KEV   As he steps up.
        Man enough to be a man

BEN   Amongst all these boys

KEV   No surprises

BEN   As he walks calmly through the team

KEV   Takes off the white Nike headband

BEN   That holds back his perfect hair

KEV   And he doesn't even break a sweat

BEN   As the scatter of the few parents who could be arsed
        to come
        Fall silent on the touchline

KEV   And the centre back of the other team looks away

BEN   Hiding his tears

KEV   From his peers.

BEN   And she turns to us…

         She turns to us…

JACK   Us.

BEN   Our best friend

JACK   Our only friend.

BEN   She turns to us and says

LISA   *What's his name?*

BEN   And now
         Things
         Won't
         Ever
         Be
         The same.

KEV   As the universe stops for everyone.
         Everyone except one

LISA   But that's not today.
         That's his day
         And today's not his day
         / Today's my day
         Always will be

JACK   Today's my day.
         Always will be.

BEN   On that one bit of grass left in our town
         That they can't rip up and build some new flats for the
         Bozos on.
         The field.

KEV   Where boys became kings
         Where boys became lions

JACK   Where boys became…

KEV   The football and the girls
       The shouts and the thrills
       The being young and not thinking to care

BEN   The field

KEV   Far away now.
       Twenty years

BEN   Still close

KEV   Always.

BEN   / That day.

KEV   That day.

       She says…

       She says –

LISA   No.
       She said –

KEV   She always said I was it
       Innit.
       I was all that mattered

LISA   And that matters
       Round here

KEV   Round here
       That matters.

       So I waited
       By the gate
       The school gate
       Three thirty

LISA   *Don't be late*

KEV   She said.
       Same time

LISA   Same place
       As always.

Car parked up on the curb.
Knowing that it will drive the teachers to fuckries
Knowing that it will get me shit tomorrow in form class
Knowing that it will make me
The talk
Of the changing rooms.
Knowing that I love it
Him.

KEV   But at the gate

LISA   The school gate

KEV   Three thirty
Same time

LISA   Same place

KEV   She ain't there.

And it ain't a panic attack.
It ain't ants climbing over my skin
Butterflies hatching in my guts
Just a little wander of my brain.
A little side to side.
She's young you know
She's pretty
She's...

So a little side to side
Ain't like
It ain't happened
Before
Natural.
So out comes the Bennies
Out comes the Clipper
And the soft passage of smoke relaxes
The taxing
Situation
That's creeping up on me
At half past three
At the school gate

LISA   Because I ain't there.
And that's a surprise

KEV   So after a quick refreshment on behalf of Mr Hedges
        It's in the motor
        Seat belt on
        Dump valve bleating through the gears
        Speed bumps just the
        Ying
        To my suspension's
        Yang.

        Round the garages
        Maybe...
        Just maybe.

        She's young
        She's pretty
        Of an age when...

        Too pretty for me.

LISA   But round the garages is just a group of wankers
        From Year 7.
        Thinking they're cool
        Smoking the butts left by our lot after school

        But I shouldn't –

        What?
        What are you looking at?

BEN   I was just a kid.

LISA   And?

BEN   Jack ain't bad
        Bad enough
        To know me
        Not like I'm bad
        Not proper.
        I got bollocks though
        And bollocks count for something

JACK   But Colville Close is small

BEN   It's close

JACK   And you grow up
          Day by day

BEN   Year by year.

JACK   And as you get bigger

BEN   So does Jack

JACK   So it's obvious really

BEN   So obvious

JACK   So obvious it's more than obvious

BEN   You have to be mates

JACK   Best mates
          Live-in-each-other's-skin mates.

BEN   So when you go up to Seniors

JACK   Who do you walk with?

BEN   And when you get put in the same class

JACK   Who do you sit with?

BEN   And when the fit girls go for the popular lads instead
          of you?

JACK   It ain't your fault.

BEN   The popular lads call you a faggot and a nonce
          For hanging round with a faggot and a nonce

JACK   They're just pricks ignore them.

BEN   And instead you just hang around with your bad mate
          Your weird mate
          Ben.

JACK   You ain't a bad lad.

BEN   But maybe I am.

          So it's simultaneous alarm clocks

JACK   Two Shredded Wheat

BEN   Uniform ironed

JACK   Hair slicked back

BEN   And neat.

JACK   Ben waiting outside my door
        Quarter past eight
        Every day.
        Walking to school together

BEN   With your only mate.

JACK   *What's up with your shirt?*

BEN   *Nothing.*

JACK   *Look like you've been fucked through a hedge
        sideways.*

BEN   Keep quiet
        Keep schtum
        Don't let him know

JACK   *Ben?*

BEN   Not even nine in the morning
        And it's already begun.

        Think
        Columbine
        Think
        Virginia Tech
        Think
        Sandy Hook
        Then breathe.

        Think
        Tony Wicks
        His gang of pricks
        An AK…
        A filleting knife…

JACK   *You alright?*

BEN   *Yeah come on
        Let's leave.*

KEV   Lids open
       Sun's up already
       Curtains split
       By the human alarm clock
       That is my old tit.
       Clock gives it that I'm late
       Give it right back.
       Blue skies
       Be no work today
       Reebok Classic of a day today.
       Morning radio chirps out
       Some banging
       Two step sounds
       And the day beginneth.

LISA   Ring Kerry
       Before I text him
       To tell him
       That I'll let him
       Tonight.
       She's laughing
       Lol.
       Saying
       'Why tonight?'
       'What's the occasion?'
       That maybe I love him
       I say
       'Like we love them all'
       She says back
       With a wisecrack
       She must think is some kind of wisdom.
       Coming from the girl who's more akin
       To a leg up round the alleyway
       On lunch
       Than this love hunch that my heart's producing
       With its flutters
       And its beat-skipping.
       So I just say
       Jealous?
       And she says
       'Yeah'

And I say
Today's the day
Why not?
Why wait?
Today's the day.

And she says
'I tell the other girls then yeah?'
And I say
Don't...
And she says
'Why not?'
And I say
Because this is special
And she says
'You're special'
And I...

KEV   Pick up my phone
To bleat the usual excuse
Of bad stomachs
From bad kebabs
From bad night outs
In bad streets.
But the phone's started up without me
Bleeping its bleep in my hand
Ignoring my finger's request.

And it's her.

The one thing that saves this life
From being just another
Bad cover
Of all the other lads that grew round here
Before I.
In capital letters she speaks to me
Important like.
And it's the news
'TODAY'S THE DAY'
She says
Today's the day
Yes it is
Reebok Classic of a day today

Yes.
It.
Is.

LISA   And the line goes dead.
        Cut off.
        Indefinitely.
        And the dialling tone seems to be laughing a little bit
        And I think about the consequences
        And all that other shit
        That people say to think about.
        Not that it matters
        Not now…

        Text
        Sent.

JACK   So it's lonesome travels to school

BEN   In company of two

JACK   Turn right out of Colville
        Past the terraced houses

BEN   Built to cage our class
        Sold to us on the cheap
        So we never thought to ask
        For anything more than an industrial nine till five

JACK   Come home
        Watch Match of the Day
        Down ten Stellas

BEN   And smash up our wives.

JACK   But that ain't us.

BEN   Not
        Yet.

JACK   So just carry on.
        Same as every day
        Whiling the hours away

BEN   Cut initials into each other's skin
        Let it bleed
        Into one.

JACK   Private chat

BEN   For private lads

JACK   Create our own language
For our own stories.
Separate from all that shit at school

BEN   No chance of fitting in with the cool
Clique.
Who live to speak
Their ill words
And think
Their ill thoughts
That comprise of cusses
That have no answer or retort

JACK   'You're fucking sad'

BEN   Yeah.
I am.

But I've got you

But I've got you

But I've got you Jack…

Mate…

JACK   *Yes mate?*

BEN   *Tony Wicks…*

JACK   *He's a bell-end.*

BEN   *Yeah.*

JACK   *Just another football-team wanker.*

BEN   *Yeah.*
But –

JACK   *Ignore him.*
I told you before.

BEN   *He said he's gonna smash me up.*

JACK   *What?*

BEN   *Tonight.*
          If I don't get him twenty quid.
          He's the one who fucked up my shirt.

JACK   *Fuck.*
          What you gonna do?

BEN   *Dunno.*

JACK   *I could probably nick some money off my mum?*

BEN   *Yeah?*

JACK   *Yeah.*
          But not by tonight.

BEN   *I'm dead.*

JACK   *He was probably just talking shit.*

BEN   *Nah.*
          He said.

          I was thinking about telling –

JACK   *No.*

          And his eyes get that sad Bambi look
          Coz he knows
          Like I know
          That all it'll do
          Is push the knife in slow.
          Because that's the way it is round here
          And that's the way it'll stay.
          You're either one of the popular lads
          Or you're like us

BEN   Sad
          Prey.

JACK   *We'll sort it.*
          Us.

BEN   So it's alright.
          Because it ain't big to cry
          Or try to fit in
          With the shit in
          Here.

Just join the football team
And play up front like Wicksy

JACK   Get a quick handjob
Up the park
Behind the swings
From the queens of the school
Whose lips drool at some boring story
Of Jordan's tits
Or Britney's bits
Or Christina's slit.

BEN   Different stories
For different people.

Don't speak that much
To no one

JACK   'Cept me.

KEV   Scrape myself from the bed
Sky's up there smiling
Warm and righteous.
Don't get better than this.
'Part from the cherry-balmed linger
Left from the taste of her kiss

LISA   Get to school ten minutes before the bell
Chain-smoked six fags on the way.
Marlboro Light head rush
Adds to the bad feeling my stomach's spitting up.
Push it back down.
Think of...
Excited flutters
His warm hot breath
And the mutters
Of love
Or some other such.
As his hands undress me
And this once
I will let them
Rest
Where they want to rest

> Without complaint
> Or stress

KEV   Sat on the sofa in yesterday's boxers.
         Ignoring my own smell wafting up
         And stinking at my nose.
         Roll a spliff
         Slim-skinned Rizla shakes in my hand
         Steady.
         I'm ready.
         And toke.
         Stopping the day and anything it can throw.

LISA   Morning lessons pass quietly
         Thinking about things…
         I shouldn't be thinking 'bout.
         In classrooms with teachers not much older
         Than the girls who meet down the crèche
         With equal disappointment
         Of this life
         This mess

KEV   'Bout ten start to think about

LISA   The fact that it's actually going to happen

KEV   Today

LISA   Three thirty

KEV   Can't come quick enough

LISA   Even though I'm scared

KEV   This is it

LISA   The moment
         I give it away
         To him
         Today.
         Today I'm his
         His and no one else's.

         And the boys that I might of once kissed
         While pissed
         Up the park.
         Ain't nothing to me

KEV   The girls that stank up my fingers
         On nights when I was meant to be home
         Learning.
         So I don't end up being
         What I end up being
         Ain't meaning shit to me now.

LISA   Today is the day

KEV   Reebok Classic of a day

LISA   No more V plates

KEV   No more pretending

LISA   No more innocence

KEV   No

LISA   No
         Not after today.

KEV   And I'm thinking...

LISA   His mum's out till ten tonight

KEV   Need some johnnies

LISA   Plenty of time

KEV   Want this to be perfect

LISA   No need to freak out

KEV   Want this to be better...

LISA   Everyone does this

KEV   Than anything else.

LISA   Everyone does this.
         Everyone.

         Calm
         Down.

         Then colours outside the schoolroom seem brighter
         Breath lighter.

Today's the day
My day.

JACK   On the playground
Fenced in by metal gates
And CCTV
To keep the nutters out

BEN   With their guns

JACK   And their knives

BEN   Ready to take young lives.

JACK   Stuck in a corner

BEN   Camouflaged
As normal kids

JACK   Keeping our heads down
Not playing the clowns

BEN   Just draw the attention
Of eager voices
Willing to risk a detention.
To take the piss
And punch and bite
Or kick
The confidence you're born with out of you.

JACK   Football rolls over

BEN   Flinch at its leather

JACK   Just a quick touch
See his face drop.
Doesn't expect it from me

BEN   *You prick*

JACK   As I kick it up
And catch it on my neck

BEN   *Give it back*

JACK   Flick it round onto my chest
Let gravity do the rest.
As it drops at my feet
Like it always does in my head

And it's straight back to him
Dead.

BEN   Dead.

JACK   Dead straight.
        And the lad says

        'Cheers'

BEN   And the lad says

JACK   'Wass your name?'

        Jack

BEN   Jack who's been in your class since you were thirteen

JACK   'Why don't you play for the footy team?'

BEN   Why don't you Jack?
        Someone holding you back?

JACK   Nah.

BEN   As he turns back round
        To the other world.
        To the lads
        The glory
        The girls.

JACK   'Wicksy's gonna fuck you up later you faggot'

BEN   My fists clench
        Maybe
        Maybe I could...
        Maybe
        Just maybe...

        Think
        Columbine
        Think
        Virginia Tech
        Think
        Sandy Hook
        Then breathe.

        Think –

JACK   *Let it go, Ben.*

BEN   Always let it go.
        Fucking prick
        Show him one day.

        Life is just the blanks I don't hear
        And the words they call me
        Prick
        Paedo
        Queer

JACK   *LET IT GO!*

BEN   *What's it matter to you?*

JACK   *I'm your mate*

BEN   Bell goes
        We're already late.
        Science with Mr Cobb
        Looks like Jesus
        Or some other religious knob.

JACK   Just sit down in anonymity
        Remember our place in the school hierarchy
        Quiet boys.
        Quiet boys behind tables with pictures of hearts
        with initials

BEN   Cut into their flesh

JACK   Initials of girls that'll never know

BEN   Never grow –

JACK   To beat
        In synchronicity.

        So sat in biology
        In the front row

BEN   Back taken already

JACK   Ben and Jack sit
        In the shit

BEN   Like any other day in a mixed-ability class
Where to pass
Is all that's asked.

JACK   Mr Cobb's smiling

BEN   Smiling his Jesus smile
Right under his beard

JACK   'Today is dissection'

BEN   His voice bangs out

JACK   'No room for the squeamish'

BEN   His voice celebrates in its glee

JACK   'If anyone would like to sit out?'

BEN   His voice angles itself
Directly
At me

JACK   'Just raise your hand.'

BEN   And what with the two fat girls

JACK   Who in another world might be your mates

BEN   Walking out

JACK   You know there ain't no way now

BEN   No way

JACK   'Less your gay?

BEN   That you're leaving this room.

JACK   'What are we cutting open, sir?'

BEN   The Captain Cock of the Football Team
Tony Wicks splutters
Thinking his mutters make him the hard man of
the class

JACK   'Is it another eye?'

BEN   Thinking his love of all things filth stand him out.
Thinking this is another time to prove he's the man

That all the girls want to fuck
And all the lads want as a mate
Coz he can bend a ball like Beckham
And his mum lets him stay out late

JACK   'No Tony.
Not today.
Today we have something a bit bigger'

BEN   And there it sits
In a Tesco's bag
Little bit of brownness
On the white plastic
That lets you know its contents
Are horrific.
As Cobby pulls the bag back
It reveals itself to the ready audience
As wet as the abattoir floor
A pig's decapitated head
Who could ask for more?

JACK   'How's that for you?'

BEN   The pig smirks the smirk of the dead
The gone
The absent

JACK   'Now who wants to help with the first cut?'

BEN   Look down
Don't stand out
Don't look like you want it
Don't look like you want to do it
Don't look like you need it

JACK   'Get Tony to do it
He's good with his hands'

BEN   Kerry screeches
One of the slags in the back row
One of Tony's regular bitches.

JACK   'Ben the faggot.
He like pigs, sir.
Get him to do it'

BEN   Cobby doesn't even think of a reprimand
        The Captain has spoken
        And his law
        Will be met

JACK   'Yes, Ben.
        Come on down'

BEN   Their laughter and smirks fill the room till all the
        oxygen is gone. I stand there with my audience waiting
        for me to fuck up or be sick. To make a dick out of
        myself so I can become the next anecdote they can tell
        at lunch or break time. A new nickname for the kid in
        Year 10. Which one? You know the one with the pig.
        The weird one. Bacon Frazzle.
        This will last.
        This.
        Will.
        Last.

JACK   Cobby hands Ben the chisel
        And explains how a hammer blow
        Will crack the skull
        And let him in.
        Don't fuck it up
        That's what I think
        Don't fuck it up and drag me down with you

BEN   Hear their words before they are said. Curse my mum
        for not buying me the shoes that would make me fit in.
        Curse my shirt for having a cardboard collar instead of
        a soft one that would make me fit in. Curse my feet for
        not being able to kick a football. Because that's what
        matters round here.
        I.
        Wish.
        They.
        Would.
        All.
        Stop.

Take the chisel
Take the hammer
And it's easy
No stammer.
Split the skull in one quick hit
First girl holds her mouth
To keep in the sick.
But that ain't enough

JACK   And he's bringing it down again
And again
And the girls are running for the door
And the smirks on the cool kids' faces
Ain't so smirky
No more

BEN   Can't stop
Can't stop the hammer
The blood
The release.
And the pig
The pig…

Could be any of them
All of them.

Think
Columbine
Think
Virginia Tech
Think
Sandy Hook
And breathe.

Think
Cold metal
Tearing through flesh
You asked for this
Bleed.

JACK   Cobby's hand on Ben's
Brings the latest Tarantino spin-off
To an end.

BEN   When Cobb stops me the pig's a mess

JACK   Ben comes and sits back down next to me

BEN   Cobb don't say a word.
Just quietly moves the pig's head under the lab table.
Easy life
Why bother with the mentally unstable?

JACK   'Get your textbooks out and turn to page twenty-three'

BEN   Cobby says looking at me

JACK   'As Ben has ruined the practical'

BEN   Like he can see something in me
Like he understands something.
He doesn't understand shit
And he never will.

Tony Wicks meets my eyes

JACK   'You're dead after school.
You fucking weird scumbag'

BEN   Is all he can say.

Pig eyes
Pig face
Pig mouth
Pig talk
Is all I see.
When he looks across the classroom
When he looks across at me.

JACK   The class are all staring
And I'm doomed
By association.

Ben tries to say something in my ear
But I can't stand it any more
The dank poisonous air
Of having him near.

BEN   *Mate…*
Mate…

Please, mate…

JACK   Hand up.
Just need to get away from him.
My mate.
Blood lacing his too-pale hands
His too-neat fingernails
His too-calm eyes.
Just need…
To get…
Away.

LISA   After break.
Word's spreading
Like it's something
That's gonna change everything.
Forever.
And suddenly I'm not feeling so clever

KEV   Sitting at home
Thinking it over
Me and her
The girl that I've waited
To let me

Be
Completely
With her.

Now it's here
Now the fear

LISA   He's older

KEV   She's younger

LISA   More experienced

KEV   Popular

LISA   And he used to be…

KEV   Like I used to be…

LISA   Then Kerry texts me to say…
That she had to say

KEV   And it might stop the lads at work thinking I'm gay

LISA   And now the sixth-formers know

KEV   The clock's hands
Tick, tick, tick
Slow

LISA   And I wish she didn't

KEV   And I know she's young

LISA   Because if the teachers knew…
They'll think I'm

KEV   Too young

LISA   One of them girls
That never escape at the station
Just one of them girls
That's known only by reputation.

So I text Kerry.
Say
What the fuck!
I'm not just some story for her to spread
Sniggering Year 12s

Picturing me in bed.
She texts back.

'What you saying?
As if it's even a big deal.'
I can hear her voice
That high-pitched
Slag
Squeal.

Then I get it.
I finally get it.

She thinks we're the same.

KEV   So I pick up keys and dress
In to the car to unwind
De-stress.
Windows open
Tunes loud.
My voice mimics lyrics
Chatting 'bout antics
Of the streets
And peeps
Just like me.

This life holds no truth
But the booze
Birds
And laughs
That come with unemployment
Spliff
And craft.
Bassline singeth out
And the local kids flick their chins
As I pass
The King…

Of all who's left

LISA   But I can't leave it.
I can't
Be having
That.

You're bang out of order.
I write back
Fingers smashing at the phone's keypad
Almost opening up a crack

'You always did think you were better than us'

KEV   Twelve-year-olds impressed with a fast car
An older lad that never travelled that far
From this shitty little town.
Come shitty little city.

LISA   And I wanna say…
Yeah.

KEV   Where you are what you score on the fairground
punchbag
Status measured by the tally of lads
You filled in
When you were kids.

LISA   I am better than you.

KEV   Never forgetting
That once…

LISA   But that would be my downfall.
The end of my so-called
Popularity.
My biological windfall.

KEV   Once…

LISA   But
I want
Her
To understand.
This isn't like her and Tony Wicks
And the rest of the football team

KEV   Once…

LISA   The pinnacle of any pre-college wag's dream.

KEV   You used to be something.
Something more.

LISA   I haven't already become a regular
        For all the lads
        Waiting for extras
        To star in their next mobile-phone premiere
        Over the park
        A red carpet
        Leading you into the dark of the bushes.
        And you can't even make out
        Which one it is
        That you're with

KEV   Now there's just…
        Her.

        Someone that might matter.
        Someone that could do better.
        Someone who makes this life
        Worth
        While.

LISA   Fake a smile.
        It'll be over soon.

KEV   Let the throttle down
        Dump valve cuts through the morning air
        Distracting
        The feeling
        Sneaking
        Up inside my guts.

        I'm going to take it
        Take it from her
        And I'm just another waster

LISA   Kev's not like that

KEV   She's young
        Clever
        Pretty.
        Soon be off to college
        Then university

LISA   Kev's special

KEV   Far from me
        And this shitty little town

Come shitty little city.
Where your only hope is of escape
To somewhere they can't remember your name
And chances are you won't be back again
To see what you left.

LISA   Turn off the phone.
Breathe.

But it's not enough.

The boys are looking at me with leers
And the smart girls meet me with knowing stares.
So I'm hand up and toilet-bound
Got to get out of this greenhouse classroom
Not waiting for the teacher's voice to release a sound
Get into the corridor
Make my way down the hall
Need some air
Need it all.

JACK   *Lisa!*

LISA   *Jack.*

JACK   *Where you going?*

LISA   *Toilet. You?*

JACK   *Yeah, going for a slash*

LISA   *Cool*

JACK   *What class you in?*

LISA   *Geography*

JACK   *With bender Harris?*

LISA   *Yeah*

JACK   *He is well gay*

LISA   *Yeah, yeah he is*

JACK   *You heard about Wicksy and Ben?*

LISA   *No.*

JACK   *Said he's gonna smash him up tonight if he don't get him twenty quid.*

LISA   *Really?*

JACK   *Yeah*

LISA   *He's only saying it.*

JACK   *Nah.*
        He's a prick to Ben.
        Always has been.

LISA   *He's not like that.*

JACK   *Maybe not to you.*

LISA   *What's that meant to mean?*

JACK   *You know.*

LISA   *We're mates Jack.*
        That's all.

JACK   *Nice mates.*

LISA   *I can have a word with him.*
        If you like?

JACK   *As if that's gonna make it better.*

LISA   *What do you want me to do then, Jack?!*
        Go on, tell me?
        For fucksake.

        I'm sorry.
        I didn't mean that.

JACK   *Are you alright?*

LISA   *Yeah.*
        Why?

JACK   *You look like you're gonna cry.*

LISA   *I'm fine.*

JACK   *If you wanna talk about something, it's okay.*
         I mean, I know we ain't like what we used to be.
         Back in the day.
         But –

LISA   *I'm good, Jack.*
         Honest.

         I better go.

JACK   *Lisa…*

LISA   *Yeah?*

JACK   *You remember when we tied that fishing line from one*
         side of Colville to the other coz Ben said it was so
         strong it would cut a car in half and you said that's
         bollocks so he tied it up from one lamp post to the
         other across the street and we all just sat there shitting
         ourselves waiting for a car to come.

         You remember that?

LISA   And my brain itches…
         Searching for the memory…
         Was that me?
         My life?

         Then Ben's dad came down the road and he started
         crying and the car just snapped the line and he
         wouldn't have even noticed if it weren't for Ben
         flapping his arms about and acting all weird.

JACK   *Yeah!*

LISA   *I hadn't thought about that for ages.*

JACK   *It was well funny.*

LISA   *Yeah.*
         Yeah it was.

JACK   And she smiles

LISA   Just like / I used to.

JACK   She used to.

And I think…

I think…

I…

LISA   *See you around, Ja–*

JACK   *Do you wanna bunk this afternoon with me?*

LISA   *What?*

JACK   *This afternoon.*
Do you wanna come over the field and get stoned I've
got some draw we could get caned it would be cool
a laugh yeah.

LISA   *Yeah*
Yeah, why not.

I say it.
Anything's got to be better than waiting here in school
No longer protected
By the cool
Clique.
As suddenly the ill words they speak
Are of me.

And the gear might make it easier
With Kev
He's a big fella
And Kerry said it hurts
In a good way
The first time.
Then you're fine to do it again.

So a bit of gear might help me
Relax
De-stress
And make it more special

Is Ben coming?

JACK   And I wanna say no.
       I wanna say can't it just be us?
       Just be me?
       For one day
       Forget about Ben
       Pretend.

       Then I see Ben in class on his own
       Walking home on his own
       Blood staining
       Bullies caning
       Head caving
       In.
       Emotional scars lining the skin.

       And I think

       I think.

       I think what if…
       What.
       If.

       Yeah Ben as well

LISA   *Little reunion.*

       And he looks at my tits.
       And I think he must know.
       And I want to run
       Run and run and run and run.

       But the world has stopped today
       Now it moves so slow.

       So I ignore his look
       This boy that I've know all my life.
       And he just says

JACK   *Meet me at the field*

LISA   *I'll slip out the gate*

JACK   *Twelve thirty*

LISA   *Don't be late*

JACK   And I say

> *Yeah, course.*
> *Wicked*

Maybe…
Just maybe…
This could change it all.

Today could be the day
The day when it all goes right.
And then we can hang around with other lads
That ain't stuck down Colville Close
For their lives.
Other lads
Who play for the football team
And have older mates who drive fast cars

KEV   It's around noon now
And I'm trapped in a café
Grease dripping
From the walls
Plates
Clientele.

And it's just the smell of sausages
And bacon
That's fucking with my stomach
Turning it upside down.
Inside out.

Just the smell…

Coz the day is halfway through
And I have achieved fuck-all
But to buy protection.
But then what is that on any other day
Just while the hours away
Counting the clock's ticks
And tuts
Reminding me that what I ended up
Ain't much.

'Usual is it Kev?'

The waitress shouts from behind the till
A woman who quite obviously
Has already had her fill.

'You see his picture up there?'

She turns to one of the punters
Fresh from the bookies' for a meal
A fixture of this habitat
Men left to live in their own swill

'Use to be something of a big deal
Did our Kev'

Then she wanders to the framed picture that's stuck on
the wall
The boys all sat there
Round a trophy
And a ball.
The faded legends of this shitty little town
Come shitty little city

And one of them
Looks…
Like…
Me.

LISA So it's two-all
Last minute of the Cup Final
The All-Essex Cup Final
Big deal.
The pitch is heavy and wet
Kits sodden with a mix of mud
Sweat
And blood…

KEV And I'm forced to live it all over again
That story
That time
That will define
Everything I ever fucking do.

LISA And there he stands
With the heart…
Of a lion.

As the scatter of parents
Fall silent on the touchline.
And the centre back of the other team
Looks away
Hiding his tears
From his peers.
Then...

KEV   The punter looks at her with a growing scowl
Not knowing we both end up the same.
She touches the picture
Her fingers leaving a greasy stain

'Tottenham were gonna sign him
That's what they said'

And I wanna say
I'm still living
I'm still...

LISA   Here?

KEV   But I know that I'm dead.

All
That
Promise.

The lad that had the skill
Must've been born in Brazil
Made his markers look small
Spurs gagging for his squiggle
Girls moist at the way he dribbles.
Power still talking about how he played
Then how he strayed.

The one they said could make it all the way.

Just an empty space on the back page
Where my name should sit.
And a lifetime to wallow in the shit.
Not
No
More.

Three hours
Till I'm with her
Till the moment I achieve something
In this life
They can't measure
With a means test
Down the dole office
For the government's pleasure.

She changes the world
Lisa
My girl.
When she sits on my lap
And strokes my cheek.
Says that I'm a Good Guy
Sweet.

The girl with the smile
That lets you know kindness exists
It grows when she's near.
There ain't nothing to fear.

So back in the car
Drive around for a bit
Kill some time.
Change the radio station over to Magic
And listen to something warm
And shit.

And smile a smile only she knows.

Today's the day
Yes it is.
My day.

BEN   The scalpel sits in my hand
Perfectly.
Reflecting the baby face
That hides such rage

Push the blade into my skin
Just a nick.
Fucking silence that prick
Tony Wicks.

Cobb's not noticed it's missing
Too busy laughing
Just like all the others.
He knows
He's seen it all before
He knows the law
He knows this place
And how it wastes everything
Everything different.

Think
Columbine
Think
Virginia Tech
Think
Sandy Hook
Then breathe.

Think
Scared faces
Begging for life
Think
Give a fuck
Grieve.

JACK   *What you got in your hand?*

BEN   *Nothing*

JACK   *Yeah you have.*
         Come on what is it, mate?

BEN   Slide the scalpel into my pocket

         I said nothing.

         They'll wait

JACK   *Alright then*

         Anyway…
         Skip maths today

BEN   *No.*

JACK   *Skip maths today*

BEN   *No*

JACK   *Skip maths today*

BEN   *No*

JACK   *Come on*

BEN   *No*

JACK   *What are you gay or something?*

BEN   *No*

JACK   *Then come on.*

BEN   And it's easy.

         Alright

JACK   Just walk out the gate
        Past the Year 7s
        Smoking their fags badly
        Bought off some Year 11
        Sold gladly at fifty pee a hit
        For the profit
        Of his Friday night
        Laced with Hooch
        And 20/20
        Make the girls loose
        If they weren't already

BEN   And the dinner lady don't look
        She don't see.
        So me

JACK   And me

BEN   Escape.
        Past the iron gate
        That keeps us from being grown-ups
        And facing futures
        Or consequences

JACK   Skip round to
        The Field.
        Where the popular boys play footy
        And the popular girls get wet

And the popular sound
Of some popular prick
Screaming
'Ronaldo'
As he kicks a ball
Into an empty net.
That could be anywhere
In any town
In any field

BEN   But.

Not.

Not today.

The kind of girl...

JACK   That wears her blazer on hot days
Because black is slimming
Not that she needs to
Coz she's fit
Hangs about with
The popular boys.
Older Lads
Who drive cars
Too quick
And drink
But ain't sick

BEN   Like you

JACK   And you

BEN   Shut up

JACK   Cunt

BEN   I said shut up

JACK   Gay cunt

(BEN *punches* JACK *hard*.)

BEN   Sorry

LISA   So I meet them over the field
        The two boys from down my road
        That I've known ever since…
        I was ever.
        Since I found out the importance
        Of who you're with
        And where you sit
        What makes you cool
        Part of the clique.
        The rules of this school
        Playground
        World.
        The reason to become just another popular girl.

        All makes you forget
        Back then
        And your friends
        There in Colville Close.
        Where it was small
        Where it was close.

        This is nice
        The three of us
        Been ages

JACK   *Yeah*

LISA   *Your mum'd freak if she knew you were bunking.*

JACK   *Same as yours*

LISA   *My mum lets me stay out till ten*

JACK   *Not on a school night*

LISA   *Yeah*
        She does.

JACK   *She don't.*
        She talks to mine
        She says –

LISA   *Probably trying to make her feel better*

JACK   *For what?*

LISA   *Treating you like a little boy still*

JACK   *That is harsh.*
        Bitch

LISA   *Don't call me that*

JACK   *Don't act like one then*

LISA   *Just saying.*

        Why don't you come over the park?
        We all go there on Fridays.
        It's well good.

BEN   *We already do stuff on Friday nights.*

LISA   *What?*

BEN   *Stuff*

LISA   *What stuff?*

JACK   *Well…*
        We feed Ben's snake.

LISA   *You've got a snake Ben?*

JACK   *Yeah he has.*
        It's massive.

LISA   *Is it?*

JACK   *Yeah.*
        Yeah it is.

LISA   *That's a bit weird.*

JACK   *Nah it's cool.*
        You have to feed it live mice and that.

LISA   *What's it called?*

JACK   *Tell her Ben*

LISA   *Go on Ben*

BEN   *Fuck off.*

JACK   *I've told him it's not a great name for a snake but…*

        (LISA *pisses herself laughing.*)

BEN   *Fuck. Off.*

JACK   *I was only joking mate.*

LISA   *You're well funny, Jack.*

>   *You should come out with me.*
>   *Be like old times.*
>   *Up the park*
>   *It's fun.*
>   *You could come out with the football team*
>   *They all smoke weed.*
>   *You'd fit right in.*
>
>   *You were always well good at football*

JACK   *Yeah…*

LISA   *I remember when we used to play*
>   *Down Colville*
>   *Me, you and Ben.*
>   *You made us both look silly*

JACK   *You're a girl*

LISA   *So?*

JACK   *Girls are rubbish at football*

LISA   *Shut up Jack.*

>   *Fuck.*
>   *That feels like a lifetime ago.*
>   *Colville.*

JACK   *I wouldn't have got in anyway.*
>   *To the football team.*

LISA   *You could have tried out though.*

BEN   *Maybe he didn't want to*

LISA   *What, Ben?*

BEN   *Maybe he didn't want to be like that*

LISA   *Like what?*

BEN   *A cock*

LISA   *They're my friends.*

BEN   *Then what does that make you?*

JACK   *Ben!*

LISA   *I know they give you grief.*
       They're just joking

BEN   *Yeah.*
       Tony's well funny ain't he?

LISA   *I said to Jack I'd have a word with him.*
       I'll sort it.
       Promise.

BEN   *I don't want you to sort it.*
       I'll sort it myself.

       Think
       Columbine
       Think
       Virginia Tech
       Think
       Sandy Hook
       And breathe

       Think
       The scalpel
       In my pocket
       Even popular girls
       Bleed.

LISA   *You need to not take everything so serious.*
       Maybe you might get a girlfriend then

JACK   *Ben's had loads of girls*
       Ain't you Ben?

       Ain't you Ben.

LISA   *Like who?*

JACK   *Girls from St Clere's*
       We hang about with them

LISA   *Have they seen Ben's snake as well?*

        (LISA *and* JACK *are laughing*.)

JACK   *Yeah.*
        Yeah!

LISA   *You'll have to take me out some time then.*
        Show me what I'm missing

BEN   *Don't take the piss*

LISA   *I'm not.*
        Stop being a dick.

JACK   *Yeah, Ben.*

BEN   Traitor.

KEV   Brake pads stop the car
        Outside the gate
        Three twenty
        No fashionably late styling for me today.
        Just light up a Benson
        And wait.

        But as the swarm of black blazers
        Short skirts
        Platinum blonde hair
        Rush past.
        I'm left
        The last.

        She ain't there…

        And it ain't a panic attack.
        It ain't ants climbing over my skin
        Butterflies hatching in my guts
        Just a little wander of my brain.
        A little side to side.
        She's young you know
        She's pretty
        She's…

        So a little side to side
        Ain't like
        It ain't happened

Before.
Natural.
So out comes the Bennies
Out comes the Clipper
And the soft passage of smoke relaxes
The taxing
Situation
That's creeping up on me
At half past three
At the school gate

JACK   *Have a go on the bong.*

BEN   *I don't want any.*

JACK   *Go on*

BEN   *No.*

JACK   *Pussy.*

LISA   *I will*

JACK   *You sure?*

LISA   *What, don't you think I can take it?*

JACK   *No*

LISA   *Pass it over little boy*

JACK   *Don't call me that*

LISA   *Ha!!*

        (JACK *and* LISA *scuffle playfully.*)

        (LISA *pins him.*)

        Always could take you

JACK   *Only coz I let you*

        (JACK *rolls* LISA *so he's on top of her.*)

LISA   *Still beat you up if I wanted*

        (LISA *pushes* JACK *off her.*)

        Jack…
        I can see your trousers bulging

JACK   *No they're not.*

LISA   *Do you love me?*

JACK   *Shut up Lisa*

LISA   *You've got a boner.*

JACK   *No I haven't.*

         Well, what if I have?

LISA   *Maybe you can get Ben to help you out*

JACK   *Why don't you?*

LISA   *Urghhhhh Jack*

JACK   *What?*

LISA   *You're like my little brother*

JACK   *I'm two months older than you*

LISA   *Shut up Jack.*
        I've got a boyfriend

JACK   *So?*

LISA   *So I'm not like that*

BEN   *Yes you are.*
        You.
        Tony Wicks.
        Kerry.
        All the same.

LISA   *Shut up Ben*

BEN   *Everyone knows.*

LISA   *You don't know what the fuck you're talking about*

BEN   *Yes*
        I
        Do.

LISA   *Yeah well at least they ain't fucking weirdos*
        Like you.

JACK   *Why you both got to be like this?*
        We're meant to be having a laugh.
        The three of us.
        Like old times.

LISA   *Pass me the bong.*

        (*He does.*)

KEV   Garages next port of call
        The social stop
        For the smokers on the way home from school.
        No joy
        No her
        And I'm freaking
        Cars scraping
        Speed bumps quaking
        As I pass through the streets
        Of this shitty little town
        Come shitty little city
        Looking for the one thing
        That makes this world right.
        Because today was the day
        That's what she said.
        Today was the day.
        Now
        It's
        Just
        Filled
        With dread.

LISA   *I feel caned*

JACK   *You smoked too much*

LISA   *I can handle it*

BEN   *Obviously not.*

LISA   *I don't know why I even bothered coming over here
        with you.*

BEN   *I do*

LISA   *Stop being weird, Ben.*
        You're freaking me out

BEN   *Why don't you just fuck off then Lisa?*
        Why are you even pretending we're still friends?
        We ain't.

JACK   *Don't say that*

BEN   *Ever since you got with him.*
        Ever since –

KEV   So it's two-all
        Last minute of the Cup Final.
        The All-Essex Cup Final

JACK   That doesn't go here.

KEV   The pitch is heavy and wet
        Kits are sodden with a mix of mud
        Sweat
        And –

JACK   THAT DOESN'T GO HERE.

LISA   The first time I saw you
        The first time
        I felt it.
        A secret.
        That was just mine.

        Maybe –

KEV   No.

LISA   Maybe.

KEV   I love y–

JACK   *Can we all just chill out.*

BEN   *We ain't nothing to you now.*
        We never were.

LISA   *I've known you since we were kids.*

BEN   *What does that matter?*

LISA   *I care about you Ben.*
        That's why I said I'd have a word with –

JACK   *Prove it.*
        Kiss him.

LISA   *What?*

JACK   *Kiss him.*
         With tongues

BEN   *What?!*

LISA   *I've got a boyfriend Jack*

JACK   *He don't have to know*

BEN   *Shut up, Jack*

JACK   *Go on*

LISA   *Why?*

JACK   *Just do it*
         Please.

BEN   *Jack, shut up!*

JACK   *You don't understand.*
         It would make everything –

LISA   *Do you want to watch?*
         Is that what you like, Jack?
         That turn you on?

         Youse two gay or something?

BEN   *I AIN'T GAY*

LISA   *Then what are you?*

JACK   *Ben…*

BEN   *You think I'm a joke?*
         That what you think?
         You're the fucking joke.
         You slag

LISA   *Don't call me that.*

BEN   *It's true ain't it?*

         Feel the scalpel in my hand
         Maybe…
         Just maybe…

(BEN *starts to approach* LISA.)

Look at you.
A fucking pig.
With your pig eyes
And your pig smile

(*He screeches like a pig.*)

You hear me Lisa?

(*He screeches again.*)

LISA   Can we stop now.

        Kev?

JACK   No.

LISA   *You two are fucking weirdos.*
        I should never have come here.

BEN   My hand goes limp.
        And the grip
        Slips.

        Pussy.
        You fucking pussy.
        / You fucking useless fucking pussy.

LISA   *You fucking useless fucking pussy.*
        How was I ever friends with you?
        Faggot.

JACK   *Lisa…*

LISA   Stop now.
        This isn't me.
        This isn't –

JACK   No.

BEN   *Please.*

        (BEN *sits down. He is crying.*)

LISA   *That's right.*
        Cry.
        You stupid little boy.

This isn't my life
Let's stop.
Stop.

JACK   No.

LISA   *I'm going to ruin you.*
You think it was bad before?
That was nothing.
I'm going to tell everyone.

BEN   *Tell them what?*

LISA   This isn't me.
It isn't

What happened.
That you and your little faggot mate got me over here.
Tried to get me stoned and take advantage of me.
Kev's going to fucking kill you.
And Wicksy.

BEN   *I didn't do anything.*

LISA   This isn't...

Who do you think they'll believe?
Me?
Or you?

(BEN *stands and starts to walk towards* LISA.)

BEN   *Lisa!*

LISA   *You're over now.*
Both of you.
You're dead.

(JACK *rushes after* BEN.)

This isn't me.
My life
This isn't –

JACK   Blink.

LISA   Kev looks at me and behind him are all the trophies
from when he was still at school. That's the only thing

he has in his room. His mum will be back soon
He puts his hand on my leg and starts to run his fingers
up towards my...
I place a hand on his. Stop him. He whispers
something in my ear but I'm not listening now. I'm
just looking at his trophies. So many trophies.
Plastic trophies.
Made to look like gold.
Blink.

JACK   My dad wakes me up for school. Says Ben will be
round soon. Asks me if I've finished all my homework.
Asks me if I've got my PE Kit. Asks me if I've seen
Lisa lately.
'She doesn't pop round like she used to.'
Blink.

LISA   My mum hands me a card. Kisses me and says
'You're a woman now.'
My sixteenth birthday. The world is there for me
to explore.
Blink

JACK   She stands there in the corridor. It's been ages since we
spoke. Since it became clear that me and Ben were no
longer acceptable faces to be near. I think about
approaching her. Asking how she is. Then that cunt
Kerry comes out of the girls' toilets, grabs her by the
arm and whisks her away.
On the inside of my maths book her initials are
scribbled below a Biro heart.
I cross it all out. Bury it under a wall of colour.
But it's still there.
Inside.
Blink

LISA   I walk through the school gates and see Kerry stood
there with Tony. She tries to smile but Tony already
shouts I'm a
'Stuck-up bitch'
We haven't spoken for months. I see her name on the
board when I check my results. Every single subject

a 'U'. I want to text her. But that's done now. That part
of my life.
Blink

JACK   When I hear the car screech into Colville I'm sat in the
living room with my mum and dad. It's half past nine.
They're late. She's fourteen for fucksake.
She steps out the car. He leans and kisses her full on
the mouth. She walks to her door. Smiling.
Blink

LISA   I start college and realise that you can actually have
friends who like the same music and things as you.
People who like you for who you actually are not who
you need to pretend to be. I start a part-time job in a
shoe shop to save up money for a car.
Blink

JACK   Year 9 is over. When they put up next year's class lists
I see that Ben is in every single one of mine.
I look for her name…
Blink

LISA   I just about get into uni. I was thinking about maybe
going somewhere properly far away, but then actually
moving to London seemed like something that would
be really, really fun. And I could nip back and see my
folks if I wanted to as well.
Blink

JACK   Year 8. We're at the gate. The school gate. Four
o'clock. We're late. The caretaker comes up to us. I tell
him we're waiting for our friend. He asks where she is.
'Detention?'
No. In that car over there.
He laughs.
'I think she might be a bit busy mate.'
She pops her head out of the window.
'I'll meet you later. Back on Colville'
I go to say something, but she's already disappeared
back into the car.
Blink

LISA   I watch from the front door of my university hall as my
         mum and dad get into their car. My dad turns to look at
         me as he starts the engine. I can see that he's crying.
         There is a lump in my stomach. Not my stomach. My
         chest. Like I might explode. Then they pull away. I am
         alone in the world. For the very first time. Then a girl
         with blonde dreadlocks puts her hand on my shoulder
         'You got any bog paper?'
         Blink

JACK   'What's the score?'
         Two-all
         'Who cares?'
         Ben is fucking about with his yo-yo.
         Put that away
         'Why?'
         It's not cool
         'Since when have you ever known what's cool, Jack'
         I laugh. But the cruelness in her voice cuts me in half.
         Then I hear the whistle.
         And we all turn around to look at the pitch. He stands
         there alone. By the penalty spot. White Nike headband.
         Perfect hair. Doesn't even break a sweat.
         Just him. And the ball. And now the whole world
         seems to fall...
         Silent.
         Apart from her
         'What's his name?'
         Blink

LISA   I meet a boy. He's in my Wednesday-morning seminar
         class. He uses big words and wears a dinner jacket.
         If anyone from back home could see they'd call us
         twats. But I think I like him. Even if he does dress like
         someone who's forty.
         Blink

JACK   The Year 7 disco finished about an hour ago. I said
         to Ben that we were all gonna walk home together
         but he's proper paranoid now about someone smashing
         him up again. It's like they can smell it on him.

That fear. That weakness. We get to the corner of
Colville. And I can feel time passing too quick. And
I say
Lisa…
And we stop walking.
And she looks at me.
'Yeah?'

And everything is now. Everything. My whole fucking
life. And my heart is beating so fast that I think I might
vomit. And my pits are drenched. And my mouth
won't seem to say the words.

Say
The fucking
Words.

'What?'

Nothing.

And it's gone.
Blink.

LISA   He asks me if I want to come out for a drink and we do
and it's lush and then we go back to his and he asks me
if I've ever slept with someone before and I lie and say
I have. He looks so sad I tell him the truth. And then
we do it. Together. For the first time.
Blink

JACK   It's the last week before the end of the holiday. We sit
in the middle of Colville. The three of us. Ben starts to
go on about how he's freaking out about going to
Seniors. And Lisa says that she's worried we won't be
in the same classes. But I just say
None of that matters.
We'll always be friends.
Always.
And I mean it.
I really do.
Blink.

LISA   I graduate with honours. The boy is there with me.
        We hold hands and he tells me that we will always be
        together.
        Always.
        Blink

JACK   I'm sweating.
        'You first'
        She says.
        Ben has gone that weird pale colour he goes when he's
        nervous. She looks at me expectantly. I pull my white
        Adidas trousers down. And stand there with my two
        best friends. My only friends. Looking at me. I pull
        them up.
        Now you.
        She puts her hand on the zip of her tracksuit top.
        I breathe in.
        Blink

LISA   We rent a small one-bed place in Archway. It's pretty
        grimy. But it's ours.
        The boy works in recruitment now.
        He used to want to be a poet.
        Blink

JACK   We arrive at the end of the road. The end of our world.
        This is it. We will escape. Just me and her. She
        swivels round to look at me and I just say I'm scared.
        And she gives me that sad look that she always does.
        The one when Ben ruins our plans. Then she leans in
        and kisses me.
        Soft.
        On the mouth.
        Blink.

LISA   It starts as a stupid conversation when we are drunk
        one night down the pub. I say we don't have enough
        money. That our jobs aren't good enough. He says that
        no one ever thinks they're ready. That no one ever
        thinks they have enough money.
        Then he smiles.

'Could be fun trying.'
Can we do this?
Can I?

He takes my hand.
And I nod.
Blink

JACK   The door of the house next to mine opens. Ben doesn't
even notice, he's still putting ants into the jar. She walks
nervously onto the street.
I can feel my heart
Beat
Faster.
As she walks over to us she looks like she might cry
But fights it back.
She's stronger than us.
Even then.

'My name's – '
Blink.

LISA   Simone rings up from reception saying there's been
a delivery for me. Can I come and sign for it. I try and
get her to just fake my signature and use the pregnancy
line, but she is a complete and utter cow and has none
of it.

'If you can't actually work then you shouldn't be in.'

Twat. I walk down the back stairs and nip out for a
crafty fag through the fire doors. I've been trying to
quit, I really have. But the odd one here and there
won't do anything. I think. I hope.

After the fag I do a kind of weird half-jog into
reception where Simone is sat already primed giving
me an evil for how long it's taken me to get there. She
makes a comment about the fact I stink of fags and
also that I was late in this morning, but I shrug her off
and ask where the delivery is. She points, and I see the
guy stood outside with a box.

He looks just like…
Just like…

Blink

JACK   And suddenly I can hear.
Sound is everywhere.
Screams and shouts.
Breathless panting.
I'm wet.
Covered in blood and shit and piss.
'He's perfect' my mum says.
'My perfect baby boy'

But am I?

Am I really?

Is it there?

Was it there already?

Even then?

Was it always there?

All / my life

LISA   My life.

Just / blink

JACK   Blink

LISA   And you missed it.

(JACK *shoves* BEN *out of the way and surges at* LISA.)

(JACK *grabs at* LISA.)

Get the fuck off me you fucking weirdo.

(*She pulls her arm away hard. Faces him.*)

Don't ever talk to me again.
Ever look at me.
You couple of stupid fucking faggots

JACK   *Stop saying that.*

BEN   And there's moments
Moments in someone you knew
As they grew
Different from you.

Now they change
And in their eyes
Everything's
Everything's...

And you're lost in that.
That look.

As it stops being just a laugh
Just messing about

LISA   All gone.

BEN   So fast.

LISA   As you move from present
To past.

(JACK *puts his hands over* LISA*'s mouth, she squirms and her struggling shouts can still be heard.*)

(JACK *sees a plastic bag on the floor among other detritus and litter. He grabs it.*)

(*He pushes the plastic bag over her head and holds it there. Tight.*)

(BEN *does nothing.*)

(LISA *struggles.*)

(JACK *holds the bag around her head.*)

(BEN *does nothing.*)

(LISA *struggles.*)

(BEN *looks away.*)

(*This goes on for an uncomfortable amount of time.*)

(LISA *falls to the floor.*)

(JACK *sits down next to her. He touches her face.*)

(*A long silence.*)

(JACK *turns to* BEN, *who has remained still during the whole act.*)

JACK   *Mate…*

        Mate…

        Please, mate…

BEN   Too late.

KEV   And it's getting dark
       And my petrol's on red
       She ain't nowhere to be seen
       Wish she was…

       So I go home
       Eat Mum's dry chicken
       Go to bed early.
       Listen to some shit sad music
       To go with the shit sad feeling
       That's kneeling
       On my chest
       Forget the rest.
       And tomorrow's another day
       Just like the one that past
       And it won't be the last

       Keep telling yourself…

       Keep telling yourself…

BEN   Keep telling yourself that it didn't happen
       Keep telling yourself you weren't there
       And now you're running
       Like in PE
       But this time
       With a purpose.
       And your mum won't look you in the face
       And your school start to advertise your place
       And the police ask questions 'bout your taste
       In music
       And all that other clichéd shit
       That might be a reason.

But there's none.
None.
Just the memory...

Just the name that was blanked out
In the local rag
As they won't shame the young
Even after what you've done.
You keep that shame

KEV   Keep telling yourself

BEN   You were just bunking school with your mate
That you've known all your life
And they probably thought it would be a scalpel
Or a knife

Not a bag.

But not...
Not that day.

And they'll say that you should have noticed
And they'll say you should have guessed
Is that really what happened?
The papers filled us in on the rest.
Because they'll say it's obvious
So obvious
So obvious it's more than obvious...

You should never have been mates.
Best mates.
Live-in-each-other's-skin mates.

KEV   Just another car that passes the school
On the day
When kids
Stand there on ceremony.
In their black blazers
And too-short skirts
As they line the street
In memory of my girl.
The only girl...

The only thing.

The last thing...

BEN I sit at home
   Extended leave
   Not suspended
   Not expelled
   Not
   My
   Fault.

   Is it?

   Just look at the clock
   And think about the gate
   The school gate
   Twelve thirty
   Don't be late.

   Just look at the clock…
   Blink.

   Move house.
   Move schools.
   A new chance.
   A new me.
   A better me.
   Blink

   Good grades
   Opportunities
   Do I want to go to college?
   University?
   Blink

   'There's a letter for you.'
   Blink

   'Tell me your biggest secret
   Something no one else knows'
   Blink

   I'm scared
   But I put the pill in my mouth
   Peer pressure
   Till the end.
   Stomach starts to tingle about half an hour later
   The lights…
   Brighter.

The music…
Better.

And for a time…
For a time…

I forget.
Blink

'There's a letter for you.'
Blink

'We need to talk about names
What should we call him?'

Him?
A boy?
We're going to have a boy?
Blink.

A pig's head
A plastic bag.
A pig's head
A plastic bag
A pig's head
A plastic bag
Blink.

'There's a letter for you.'
Blink.

Florida
Disneyland
Just like everyone else
The crowds there
So many people
So many
Normal
People.
Blink

'You're dead after school you fucking weird scumbag'
Blink

Home owner
Mortgage

Job
A nine to five
Normality
Normality...
Blink

'There's a letter for you.'
Blink

'Drink after work?'
I can't.
'Go on'
I promised.
'One more.'
Don't forget.
'Go on.'
Don't
Forget
'Just one'
Don't forget what you are.
Blink

'Where did you get those scars on your arm?'
Blink

Don't forget.
Blink

'There's a letter for you.'
Blink

A pig's head
Blink

A plastic bag
Blink

A pig's head.
Blink

'There's a letter for you.'
Blink

Think Columbine
Think –
Blink

'Put that away'
Why?
'It's not cool'
'Since when have you ever known what's cool, Jack?'
Blink

'Wake up
You're having a nightmare.
It's over now.
It's over'
Blink.

'There's a letter for you.'
Blink

'Mummy, why is that man crying'
Blink

I'm sorry.
I'm sorry.

'I don't know what you're saying sorry for...'
Blink

'There's a letter for you.'
Blink

A pig's head.
A plastic bag
A pig's head
A plastic bag
A pig's head

(*He screeches like a pig. It goes on for an
uncomfortable amount of time.*)

Blink

'There's a letter for you.'

JACK   I don't know if you even read these letters. I hope you
        do. If I'm allowed that any more. Hope. This will be
        the last one I send. Promise. I'm getting out soon.

        I ask them questions about you. They don't say
        anything. I imagine it's the same for you. If you still
        think about me. Jack and Ben. Ben and Jack. Mates.

Best mates. Live-in-each-other's-skin mates. I wonder
if you get other friends like that. In a life. I hope not.

They're giving me a new name. A new start. A
beginning. There is no more Jack after today. Jack is
gone. No Jack here. Just a memory of a thing that
happened once. When we were kids.

I'm sorry. That's what I'm trying to say. They tell me
that it helps. To try and atone. To try and move past
this. But what is there to move past this to?

I love you.
I always did.
I'm sorry.
I.
Jack.
He.
It.

KEV   Blink.

Blink.

Blink.

Blink.

Blink.

Blink.

Blink.

Blink.

Blink.

Blink.

Blink.

Blink.

Blink.

Blink.

Blink.

Blink.

Blink…

Blink…

Blink…

Used to go out with that girl
The fit one
From Colville Close.
Used to be one of the lads
That the pretty girls at school fancied
As I was a bit hard
Then I drove the fast cars.
And when I was in Year 11
I was captain of the school football team.

And that meant something
Round here

Round here
That meant something.

Then they send you packing
And you swap your school uniform
For another one
That goes with shelf-stacking.
And the only girls
That look at you twice
Are the ones you already had up the park
White Lightning
After dark.
Breaking hymens
Ending fairy tales
On jackets laid down as bedsheets

'Part from Lisa.
Nice girl.
Our town's own little dark secret
That the kids in Year 7 tell each other
When they want to scare each other
Or make the bullies
Pause…

For a second.
Before they put your head back in that toilet full of
their piss.

(*The coloured lights of a school disco wash over
the space.*)

The only girl that knew
Once I had
The heart…

Of a lion.

(LISA *walks to* KEV. *Takes his hand. They start to
dance. It's a slow number.*)

LISA   Tell it again.

KEV   No.

LISA   Maybe next time I don't go over the field
Maybe next time it is our day.

Maybe next time I hold the bag.

Tell it again.
For us.

(*She whispers something in his ear.*)

(*He smiles.*)

KEV   So it's two-all…
Last minute of the Cup Final
The All-Essex Cup Final

BEN   Big deal –

(*Blackout.*)

(*End.*)

A Nick Hern Book

Plastic first published in Great Britain in 2018 as a paperback original by Nick Hern Books Limited, The Glasshouse, 49a Goldhawk Road, London W12 8QP, in association with Poleroid Theatre

Plastic copyright © 2018 Kenneth Emson

Kenneth Emson has asserted his right to be identified as the author of this work

Cover design by Helen Murray

Designed and typeset by Nick Hern Books, London
Printed in Great Britain by Mimeo Ltd, Huntingdon, Cambridgeshire PE29 6XX

A CIP catalogue record for this book is available from the British Library

ISBN 978 1 84842 745 7

Woodland
CARBON
www.woodlandcarbon.co.uk
NICK HERN BOOKS
Printed on Carbon Captured paper